Business & Company Resource Center

A user's guide to the BCRC

PP5W9QSPPQPDS0

DO NOT THROW AWAY THIS CODE—This is your access code to the Business & Company Resource Center. It is a unique code that gives you a 4-month access to the site.

You can access the Business & Company Resource Center from any computer with an Internet connection. Point your browser to http://bcrc.swlearning.com/ .Click the Register Your Access Code link on the left side. Once in the registration screen, hit the Register New Account button. Enter the access code shown above. After you've registered the first time, you can click the Log On button to enter the site.

SOUTH-WESTERN
CENGAGE Learning

Australia • Brazil • Japan • Korea • Mexico • Singapore • Spain • United Kingdom • United States

SOUTH-WESTERN
CENGAGE Learning™

Business & Company Resource Center:
A user's guide to the BCRC
Thomson

Executive Editors: Michele Baird,
　Maureen Staudt & Michael Stranz

Project Development Manager:
　Linda de Stefano

Marketing Coordinators:
　Lindsay Annett and Sara Mercurio

Production/Manufacturing Supervisor:
　Donna M. Brown

Pre-Media Services Supervisor: Dan Plofchan

Project Coordinator: Andretta Condon

Rights and Permissions Specialists:
　Kalina Hintz and Bahman Naraghi

Cover Image: Getty Images*

For product information and technology assistance, contact us at
Cengage Learning Customer & Sales Support, 1-800-354-9706

For permission to use material from this text or product,
submit all requests online at **www.cengage.com/permissions**
Further permissions questions can be e-mailed to
permissionrequest@cengage.com

ISBN-13: 978-0-7593-4795-3

ISBN-10: 0-7593-4795-6

South-Western Cengage Learning
5191 Natorp Boulevard
Mason, OH 45040
USA

Cengage Learning is a leading provider of customized learning solutions with office locations around the globe, including Singapore, the United Kingdom, Australia, Mexico, Brazil, and Japan. Locate your local office at **www.cengage.com/global**

Cengage Learning products are represented in Canada by Nelson Education, Ltd.

To learn more about South-Western, visit **www.cengage.com/southwestern**

Purchase any of our products at your local college store or at our preferred online store **www.cengagebrain.com**

*Unless otherwise noted, all cover images used by Cengage Custom Solutions have been supplied courtesy of Getty Images with the exception of the *Earth-view* cover image, which has been supplied by the National Aeronautics and Space Administration (NASA).

Printed in the United States of America
9 10 11 15 14

SOUTH-WESTERN
CENGAGE Learning™

Contents

Overview 1

    Stop Googling Around 2

    Features 2

BCRC Test Drive............................ 4

    Getting Started 4

    Using Additional Search Options 7

    Navigating Your Results 13

    Advanced Search 21

    Search History 22

    Search Tips 22

    InfoTrac InfoMarks 23

Using Your Research.................... 24

    Case Analysis 24

    Citing Sources in the BCRC 27

Business & Company
RESOURCE CENTER

GALE CENGAGE LEARNING

Overview . . .

The *Business & Company Resource Center*—BCRC—is an online database and research tool by Thomson/Gale. Developed for business courses in Management, Accounting, Economics, Finance, Marketing, Career Development and their related disciplines, the BCRC provides a comprehensive research center for students, instructors, and researchers in both the academic and business worlds. The BCRC meets curriculum requirements for students engaged in undergraduate and graduate work. Instructors who include the BCRC as part of their course materials do so to facilitate success in assigned research projects, presentations, cases, or outside readings. The

BCRC's home page—where you begin your search

BCRC is an especially powerful combination when used for analyzing the cases provided by Harvard Business School Publishing and other case study publishers. It is the perfect tool for courses that use assigned readings that must be timely and relevant. All readings come in full-text from such authoritative sources as *Forbes, The Economist, Wall Street Journal,* and hundreds of other publications. The BCRC also provides abstracts and complete bibliographical information for other published resources.

Student users are the focus of the BCRC and a continuing subscription to the BCRC database not only serves the postgraduate jobseeker in researching prospective employers. It is a serious business research tool when a career is underway for entrepreneurs, investors, brokers, and business strategists seeking up-to-the-minute information about their business environment.

STOP GOOGLING AROUND

Unlike ordinary search engines, the *Business & Company Resource Center* eliminates time-consuming (and even distracting) "googling" and "surfing the Web." The BCRC is the antidote to going to the Web, searching for information, and using whatever is found—the good, bad, and "Who knows where it came from?" Here is why:

- The BCRC has the depth and breadth of information needed for business courses, yet it provides more targeted and proprietary information than any Google search.
- The BCRC is very easy to use. Unlike Google, a simple company or industry search will yield wealth of indexed information—not lists of thousands of websites.
- The BCRC has the stamp of approval of the largest trusted commercial information provider in the world, Thomson/Gale.
- The BCRC offers its information in context—dynamic, accurate, and up-to-date company and industry intelligence on thousands of U.S and international companies—all powered by Thomson/Gale's robust InfoTrac system.

FEATURES

FRESH INFORMATION DAILY

BCRC sources and articles are kept current. Much of the information is renewed daily. Your professors will appreciate that the sources are legitimate and citable—and with the entire class using BCRC, it makes possible group projects that utilize a uniform resource.

As one business student noted, "I have used BCRC in conjunction with Harvard Business School case analysis and it is amazing how easy this library is to use and how perfectly suited it is to this type of research. Whether financial information, company histories, industry analysis, periodical articles, or legal issues, it is all there."

BUSINESS INTELLIGENCE YOU CAN DEPEND ON

This comprehensive database provides highly respected information sources, featuring Thomson Financial content. The variety of resources included in this database not only allows for users to research individual companies, but also supports research that compares companies within the context of their peers and industry. Unlike any other online business database available, the BCRC offers valuable access to:

- Investext® reports
- Twenty-minute delayed stock quotes
- First Call consensus estimates
- CDA/Investnet insider buying and selling activity
- CDA/Spectrum major shareholders
- Corporate chronologies and histories
- Consumer marketing data
- Emerging technology reports
- Business journal news and analysis
- Press releases

Targeted Searches and Tab Navigation
That Organize Results

The Business & Company Resource Center search forms are designed to help the user find information quickly. Company, industry, article, or advanced search options provide powerful yet easy-to-use access.

Once an initial search has been executed, the BCRC database provides an ata- glance results tab bar. Simply click on a labeled tab and view:

- Company Profile—containing detailed contact and company information
- News/Magazines—featuring relevant periodical articles
- Histories—providing a detailed history and chronology of the company
- Investment Reports—offering Investext records, analyst research reports on companies and industries
- Financials—providing in-depth detail on the company's financial standing
- Rankings—showing various company rankings within their industry and market share
- Suits and Claims—featuring civil claims filed against the company in the area of human resources
- Products—offering a complete listing of products and/or brands that a company owns or sells
- Industry Overview—detailed essays from Thomson/Gale's Encyclopedia of American Industries, Encyclopedia of Global Industries and Encyclopedia of Emerging Industries. Additional market research reports on most industries from Datamonitor International
- Associations—featuring contact information on relevant associations within the company's industry

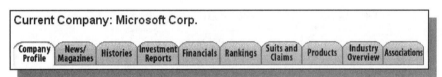

BCRC's tabbed navigation bar for a company search of Microsoft Corp.

This guide is an introduction to the BCRC database that shows you how to search for targeted information and navigate the results. In the following pages, you'll find a tutorial for the BCRC's user-friendly environment and with additional sections on using the BCRC in case study research and properly citing BCRC sources. This guide supplements the BCRC's online help, which you can always access by clicking the [? Help] link at the top of every BCRC webpage.

The BCRC is as simple to use as your favorite Web search engines—but it delivers far more.

Business & Company
RESOURCE CENTER

PL: 91 1/8 DIS: 27 7/8 K

GALE CENGAGE LEARNING

BCRC TEST DRIVE . . .

GETTING STARTED

You can access the Business & Company Resource Center with your web browser at **http://bcrc.swlearning.com/**. When prompted, enter the access code printed on the inside front cover of this guide. You will then be prompted to register. When you return to the site, you will logon with the user name and password that you created.

MAJOR SEARCH PATHS

The principal feature of the Business & Company Resource Center is how easy it is to search.

Quick Search

Just below the *Business & Company Resource Center* banner is a Quick Search bar that allows you to perform a basic search from anywhere within the BCRC database. Just perform the following steps.

1. Enter search term(s) in [Enter your search term(s): _____]

2. Select from pull-down menu to search for company, industry or articles:

    Example: Company Search Let's say you are developing a case study of the ice cream industry in the United States. You need some statistics as well as basic company information to inform your narrative. In the example, typing **Ben & Jerry's** into the quick search box yields the following results on the Company Profile navigation tab:

Results for "Ben & Jerry's" search keywords for a company

Example: Industry Description Search Let's say you are still at the BCRC home page and want to focus your research on the ice cream industry and not a particular manufacturer. You can conduct an industry description search for this, which yields SIC and NAICS industry description snapshots. If you type **ice cream** into the quick search box and select Industry Description Search from the list box, the BCRC delivers the industry descriptions that most apply to the production of ice cream from such sources as Gale's *Encyclopedia of American Industries* and *Datamonitor Industry Market Research*—often with general statistics. This kind of concise information can help with your case study narrative's introduction. (If you wanted the same

Results for "ice cream" search keywords for an industry description search

information while in Ben & Jerry's Company Profile page, click the desired SIC or NAIC codes hyperlinks.)

> **Tip**   For an industry search, you can also enter industry code, SIC or NAICS. SIC stands for Standard Industrial Classification, a system devised by the federal government that is now being replaced by NAICS, the North American Industry Classification System. NAICS was developed jointly by the U.S., Canada, and Mexico to provide new comparability in statistics about business activity across North America.

Example: Articles Search   Users can also browse journals. Focusing again on Ben & Jerry's, suppose you would like to review the introduction or reception of new products and flavors reported in the business press to further add details to your case study about the dynamics of competition in the ice cream industry. For a quick search, you would type **Ben & Jerry's** as the search string to retrieve a list of relevant articles in which the company is the topic.

Results for "Ben & Jerry's" article search

> **Tip**   The pull-down menu automatically goes back to "Company Search" after searching for articles or industry descriptions.

Quick Search Rules

To review, Quick Search bar users can search by Company, Industry, or Articles. Simply click the appropriate type of search from the pull-down menu, enter your search string and press **Enter** or click **Search**.

Quick Search will search for the following:

- Company Search—searches for matches in all company names
- Industry Search—keyword within SIC and NAICS Code Industry Description
- Article Search—searches for a particular subject in the article title. If no matches are found, the BCRC search engine will then look for the subject as a keyword assigned to the article. If no keyword matches are found, it will search for only the first word of your term or will provide a spell check—because the BCRC database "assumes" that the subject you entered could be spelled differently. If the spell check fails to find the term, a list of alternatives are suggested as shown below.

You can further fine-tune your search with the rules and suggestions given in "Search Tips," beginning on page 22.

USING ADDITIONAL SEARCH OPTIONS

The Quick Search bar is a great starting point for global searches of the BCRC database. For more focused and refined information search and retrieval, use the button bar under the heading **Additional Search Options** on the BCRC home page shown below.

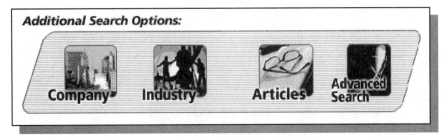

Links to Company, Industry, Articles, and Advance Search pages

By clicking on the desired search—**Company, Industry, Articles,** and **Advanced Search** discussed on the following pages—your browser will load a specialized search page on which you can refine your search with additional BCRC search options.

COMPANY SEARCH

This guided search form retrieves information based on more than just basic company name. In this search form, you may also search for companies by:

- Ultimate Parent
- Industry Code/Description, or browse for SIC Code/NAICS code
- Product/brand name or product/brand type
- Geographic location, either city or state/country
- You may also browse for companies

To begin a search from the BCRC home page, follow these steps:

1. Click the **Company hyperlink button** in the Additional Search Options bar.

The Company search form page opens in your browser.

2. Type company name in or ticker symbol (e.g., **F = Ford**).

> **Tip** If you do not know the company name, click Browse Companies link and select the desired company from the alphabetical list. It automatically enters the name into the **Company Name** text box. To return to the Company search form page without selecting a company name, click **Revise Search**.

3. Select **All Companies** or **Ultimate Parent** option.

4. Click **SEARCH** (or click **Clear Form** to start over).

The results page appears. An error page appears if the BCRC search engine cannot resolve the search with the entered data.

Company Search Options

In addition to a standard company name search, you may also search for an industry. Typing "**ice cream**" (including quotation marks as shown in the illustration on the next page) will result in all companies that manufacture ice cream. Typing the SIC code for ice cream, **2024**, yields the same results.

A search for either a company name or ticker symbol or its industry code/description can be further refined to a particular product/brand name or product/brand type or location—city and state/country—using the other options on the company search form page.

Company Search Results

Results will be returned within the Company Profile tab and/or the News/Magazine tab. (Navigating tabs is discussed on pages 16–21.) Also, the following result features appear:

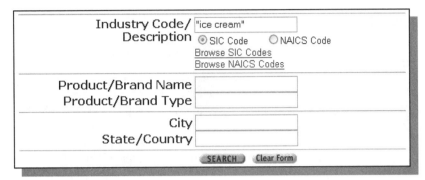

Company search form options

- Company profiles are sorted by revenue with the highest revenue appearing first.
- To view additional information on your company, select a company from the company profile result list.
- If any articles fulfill the search criteria, the News/Magazines tab will also be active.
- If no company profiles (i.e. only articles) fulfill the search criteria, the News/Magazine tab will be active; all other tabs will be inactive (shown in gray letters).

Results of "Ben & Jerry's" search with Ultimate Parent option selected

INDUSTRY SEARCH

The industry search form allows you to search for industry by SIC or NAICS code and industry description. (Recall that 2024 is the SIC code for ice cream and frozen deserts.)

> **Tip** A search for "SIC 73*" results in a list of industries in the SIC group 73. You can narrow your search by selecting one of the SIC code groups to display industry codes within the group.

Results found when searching for industry information will be found in Industry Overview, Associations, Rankings, Investment Reports, News/Magazines and Company Profile tabs. To begin an industry search from the BCRC home page, use these steps:

1. Click the **Industry hyperlink button** in the Additional Search Options bar.

The Industry search form page opens in your browser.

2. Type the **SIC** or NAIC code name in .

OR

Type description in

OR

Click either link and select the desired code.

3. Click .

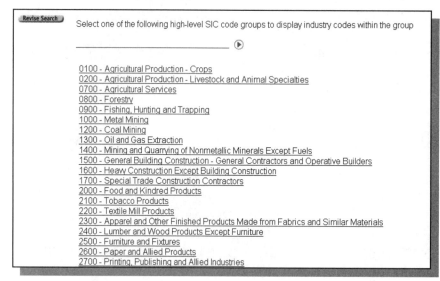

SIC Code search page—the first in a hierarchically structured industry groupings

Industry Search Results

Results from searching for industry information are shown in Industry Overview, Associations, Rankings, Investment Reports, News/Magazines and Company Profile tabs (see illustration on next page).

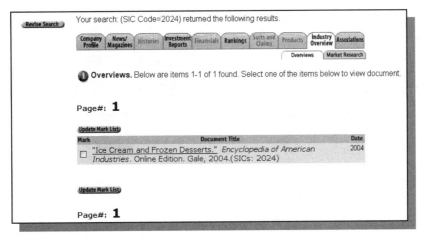

SIC Code search results page

ARTICLES SEARCH

The articles search form allows you to search for only magazine, journal, or news articles by subject, keyword, or text within the article. The Browse Journal feature allows you to select up to 10 journals to search simultaneously. You can limit your search in the search form shown below to full-text articles, peer-reviewed articles, newspapers and newswires, magazines, and journals, by journal name and date of publication. To begin your articles search from the BCRC home page, follow these steps:

1. Click the **Articles hyperlink button** 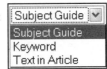 in the Additional Search Options bar.

    The Articles search form page opens in your browser.

2. Type the search term in | Search Term: Ben & Jerry's |.

3. Select the search type from the drop-down list: | Subject Guide ∨ |
    Subject Guide
    Keyword
    Text in Article

4. Click **SEARCH** (or click **Clear Form** to start over).

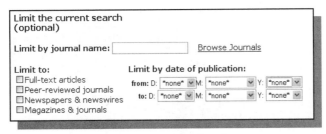

Limit the current search form on Articles Search page

Articles Search Options

On the articles search form page, under *Limit the current search*, you can limit your search to a specific journal. You can type the journal name or names in the *Limit by journal name* text box in quotation marks or select up to 10 journals from the BCRC's data base as follows:

1. Click Browse Journals.

2. Click the check box (see example below). You can check as many as 10 journals.

3. Click Update Selections.

4. Click Submit Selections.

The Limit by journal name *text box expands to show all the selected journals (see example below).*

```
                      "Dairy Farmer" OR
                      "Dairy Field" OR
                      "Dairy Foods" OR
                      "Dairy Foods Newsletter" OR
                      "Dairy Industries International" OR
                      "Dairy Markets" OR
                      "Dairy Markets Weekly" OR
                      "Dairy Record" OR
                      "Dairy Today"
Limit by journal name:
```

The articles search can also be limited by restricting your search to full-text articles, peer-reviewed magazines, newspapers and newswires, and magazines and journals. In addition, you can also specify a *from date* and *to date* by selecting from the month, day, and year list boxes.

Articles Search Results

A search for Ben & Jerry's, limited to full-text articles in 10 journals only, results in a listing of all articles in the selected journals containing *Ben & Jerry's* as a subject. You can click **View** to seearticles listed in reverse chronological order or narrow the articles by subdivision by clicking **Narrow**. You can also click to see related subjects.

Tip If you do not limit your search, your search results will appear directly on a result list page shown in the illustration on the next page.

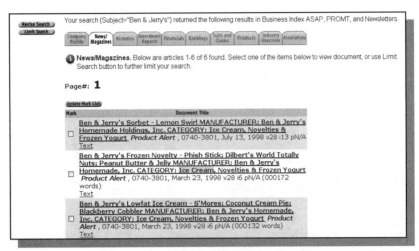

Result list page for articles subject search without limits

Searching from any Page

You can click on the BCRC navigation bar (shown larger than it is) to perform any kind of search. This bar appears on every BCRC page.

NAVIGATING YOUR RESULTS

Search results are navigated using tabs at the top of the BCRC search form. Each tab lists search results for a specific content area. The tabs are as follows for a typical company search:

- **Company Profiles** The information on this tab provides the legal and variant names of the company, its parent, SIC and NAICs codes, annual sales, employees, sales, contact information, URL, corporate officers, and so on.
- **News/Magazines** This tab lists articles related to the company and are listed by the most recent date.
- **Histories** This tab features full-text articles from *Notable Corporate Chronologies* and/or *International Directory of Company Histories*.
- **Investment Reports** This tab lists Investext reports.
- **Financials** If financial information has been made public, it will appear on this tab.
- **Rankings** Rankings published in *Business Rankings* appear on this tab as well as links to SIC and NAIC rankings for the relevant industry.
- **Suits and Claims** Articles about relevant litigation affecting a company, appearing in *Case Digests* and other publications, are listed on this tab.
- **Products** Features a table of brand names and brand types produced by a company.

- **Industry Overview**   Lists the SIC and NAICS codes that apply a company and links to their BCRC description pages.
- **Associations**   This tab also lists applicable SIC and NAICS codes.

Articles about this company
Financial Data
Legal Issues
Management
Operations & Technology
People
Products & Services
Sales & Marketing
Statistics
Strategy & Planning

Tabs become active (bold black letters) after you conduct a search. How many tabs are active depends on the level of your search results page. A company search may have only the Company Profiles and News/Magazines tabs active—but clicking on the Company Profiles tabs will show all the tabs active for which the BCRC can find relevant data. In addition to the data that applies to the company you searched, you can broaden or narrow your search to find other companies, topics, or industries by using the additional navigational tools found along the left side of the screen (see illustration at left). For our ice cream industry case study, articles relevant to Ben & Jerry's can be accessed through a navigation tool that breaks down articles into such categories as Financial Data, Legal Issues, and so on.

RESULTS LISTS: TABS AND SUBTABS

You may change the results list view to either ascending or descending order in the Company Profile tab by either name or revenue. Revenue is the default, indicted by Revenue ▼. Clicking on Company Name reorders the list alphabetically by company name. Subtabs provide better organization of results between similar content sets. They allow users to determine what type of content they wish to view. Subtabs can be found within the following main tabs:

- Rankings (tab)—Business Rankings/Market Share (subtabs)
- Industry Overview (tab)—Overview/Market Research (subtabs)

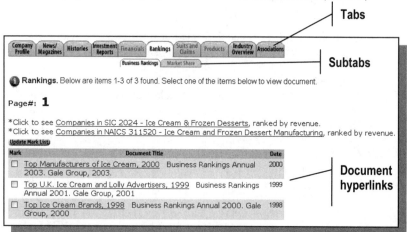

Rankings tab page for Ben & Jerry's

Additional Onscreen Prompting

Result screens will indicate if you are in company mode (Current Company) or industry mode (Current Industry). Other prompts will tell users to select a result or tab to view additional information.

NAVIGATING RESULTS SCREENS

Company Profile Results Screen

A company search may result in one or more companies. The screen below shows a search for Ford and all of its results.

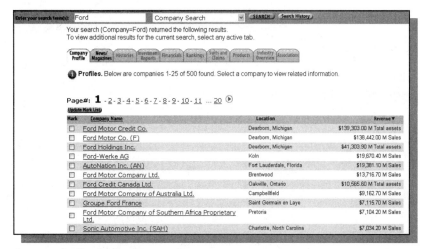

Company Profiles for *Ford* as search term

Clicking on a company in the profiles list returns that company's profile page with tabs active—shown in **bold black letters**—depending on the information the BCRC finds. From this page, users may select any tab (above) or view articles about this company by topic in the navigation tool on the left.

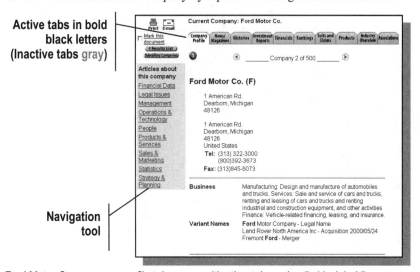

Ford Motor Co. company profile tab screen with other tabs active (in black bold)

News/Magazines Tab

Clicking the News/Magazines tab returns all articles for your search. Articles are listed in reverse chronological order with the most recent article listed first.

News/Magazines Limit Search Option   Once you've done a search and are in the News/Magazine tab you may limit your news/magazine results further by keyword, journal, date, peer-reviewed, newspapers/newswires, or magazines/journals.

PDF/Adobe Image   Full-page images are available within the News/Magazine record display. An icon on the record display will indicate if a full-page PDF is available. A simple click will launch Adobe and open the PDF. Full-page and imbedded images are available based upon rights and permission.

Ben & Jerry's News/Magazine tab screen—click on hyperlink to read abstract of article and access full text if available.

Histories Tab

Within the Histories tab are chronological and narrative histories for the company searched. The chronological histories, taken from Gale's *Notable Corporate Chronologies,* are organized in a timeline fashion that gives you an overview-style abstract of key events by year. The narrative histories, from the *International Directory of Company Histories* published by St. James Press, come in an encyclopedia-article form.

Traditionally multivolume sets only found in library and corporate reference collections, these now-online reference guides are at your fingertips in the BCRC.

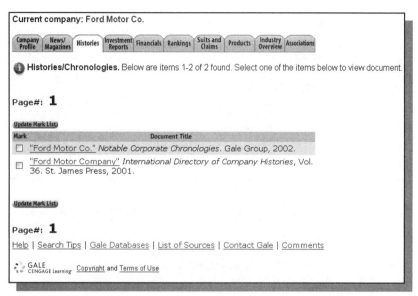

History tab screen—click on hyperlink to access a company chronology or history

Investments Reports Tab

Upon opening the Investments Reports tab, investments reports are listed for your search. The most recent reports are listed first.

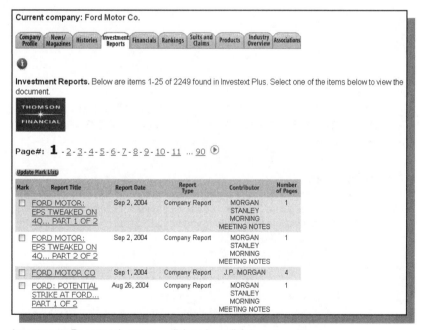

Investments Reports tab screen—click on hyperlink to access reports

Financials Tab

Current financial information is readily available. You can easily jump to view Pricing and Performance—which is updated at the close of each Wall Street trading day—four-year Annual Balance Sheet, Insider Trading, Top Institutions, Top Mutual Funds, and Top Insiders.

In the left margin you can click to view First Call Consensus Snapshot—another informative navigation tool. Also included is a link to a glossary of financial terms **Glossary** that define the various data elements found within the Company Financial and First Call Consensus Snapshot reports.

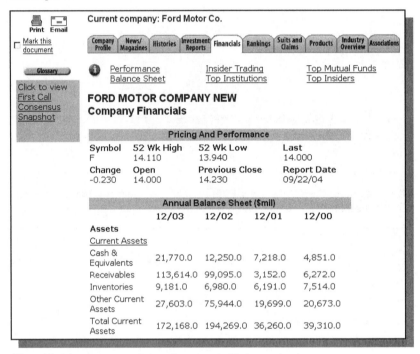

Financials tab screen—scroll down to see rest of balance sheet

Rankings Tab

The Rankings tab shows various rankings and market share tables for companies and industries from Thomson/Gale's *Business Ranking Annual and Market Share Reporter*. Information is compiled within two separate sub-tabs (when data is available), Business Ranking and Market Share.

For example, the rankings for Ben & Jerry's includes top manufacturers by market share, advertising budgets in expenditures, and ice cream sales. Such data can readily be incorporated into a table in a case study where industry comparisons are necessary to support the narrative.

To view a "peer" group list—that is, companies in the same industry— select either the SIC or NAICS link above the list of business ranking hyperlinks. This will provide a list of all the companies in the selected industry code from within the BCRC database.

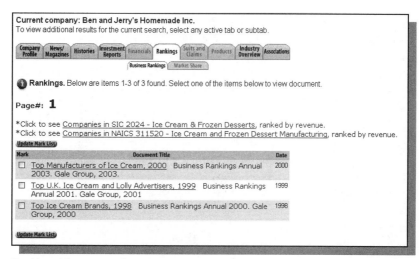

Rankings tab screen—shows a range of industry rankings for research

Suits and Claims Tab

Case digests—from *Human Resources Law Index*—are returned on the Suits and Claims tab. Click the document title link in the list to read about litigation and courtroom proceedings affecting the company being researched. Using the navigation tool (when data is available) on the left margin of the tab screen, you can click to view related subjects such as the computer software industry or employee benefits. Selecting a subject link will take you to magazine, journal and news articles on that subject.

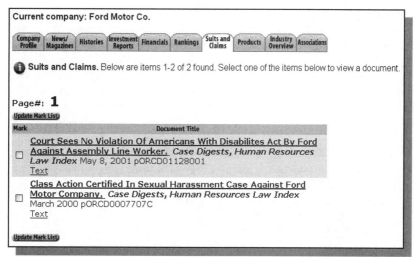

Suits and Claims tab screen for Ford Motors

Products Tab

A researched company's products and services—when available—are listed on this tab. It allows the user to quickly view products or brands by name and type. Current and discontinued products are listed in alphabetical order.

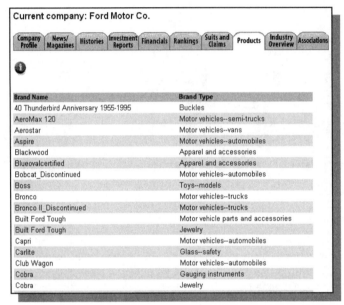

Products tab screen for Ford Motors

Industry Overview Tab/Associations Tab

The Industry Overview tab—featuring Overview and Market Research subtabs—presents the industry codes (SIC and NAICS) related to the company being researched. Selecting a code provides descriptive documents from company executive summaries, market value/volume, competitive analysis to industry statistics and the like. The Associations tab, like the Overview tab, contains relevant contact information on a company's industry associations.

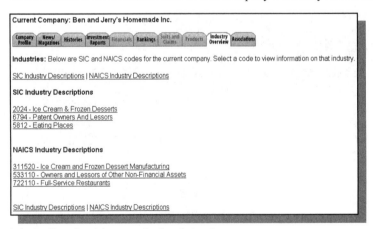

Industry Overview tab screen for Ben & Jerry's

ADVANCED SEARCH

Use this option to search for information found within specific sources throughout the BCRC. These sources appear under the same tabbed categories displayed on the navigation bar—categories that you are now familiar with after learning about the different kinds of BCRC results screens:

- News/Magazines
- Company Profiles/Products
- Histories
- Investment Reports
- Financials
- Rankings
- Suits and Claims
- Industry Overviews
- Associations

Each content area has its own advance search form page that allows you to specify keywords, dates, and other variables to search for the information you need and filtering out unneeded results. To use the Advanced Search from the BCRC home page, follow these steps:

1. Click the **Advanced Search hyperlink button** ![] in the Additional Search Options bar.

   The Advance search form page for News/Magazines opens in your browser.

2. Click the desired **Content Area** in the drop-down list:

3. Then enter the terms in the search box or boxes and select the desired field (keyword, company name, etc.) for searching from the pull-down list of index fields. Index fields and search terms may be combined by selecting the appropriate Boolean operator.

4. Enter other advanced search options as desired.

5. Click **SEARCH** (or click **Clear Form** to start over).

Note that results will only be returned from the content area selected. Availability of index fields is dependent on the content area selected.

SEARCH HISTORY

The **Search History** can be helpful if you need to go back to previous searches performed during the same session. To view the Search History, click on the Search History button in the upper right of the screen in the green navigation bar or simply scroll to the bottom of the screen and view previously searched results. The Search History is limited to 20 qualifying searches. Once you exceed that limit, the Search History starts to delete earlier searches—beginning with the first—in the list in which they were added.

SEARCH TIPS

You've already learned about searching with quotation marks around keywords. To learn more about narrowing your searches in the BCRC, click the **Search Tips** link at the top of any BCRC webpage. Here you can find out how to use search operators, enter date ranges, and use capitalization, punctuation, truncation, and wildcard characters. Two ways of refining your searches are discussed next.

Wildcards

- Asterisk (*)—matches any number of characters
- Question mark (?)—matches an exact number of characters
- Exclamation point (!)—matches one or no characters
- Boolean operators:
  - **and**
  - **or**
  - **not**
  - Parentheses: **(…)**

If you want to override the order of operators, you can use parentheses so certain terms are searched together. You can construct very powerful queries using parentheses, for example: "microsoft" AND ((federal AND breakup) OR anti-trust)

Proximity Operators

The proximity operators **W** (within) and **N** (next to) may be used to refine your search. The **W** operator will locate documents containing the specified words in the specified order within the number of words you indicate. For example, the search term "microsoft W4 netscape" finds documents that contain the word "microsoft" within four words of the word "netscape," and "microsoft" must precede "netscape." The **N** operator locates documents containing the words you specify within the number of words you specify, but the words can be in any order.

INFOTRAC INFOMARKS®

When you subscribe to the BCRC database, you not only get access to a wealth of information for your academic and professional life, you also gain a powerful yet easy-to-use tool that will save research time and help you share information with other students, instructors, colleagues, and others. An InfoMark is a stable URL, linked to BCRC online resources. It's a single-click return ticket to any page, any result, any search from the BCRC. You simply (1) right-click the URL of your search results page in your browser's Address/Location box, (2) click **Copy**, (3) place your cursor in the target document—it can be an e-mail letter, a Word document, a Web page under construction—and then (4) right-click and select **Paste**.

InfoMarks can be used like any other URL—but they're better because they're stable—they don't change. They simply update if applicable. Using an InfoMark is like performing the search again whenever you follow the link—whether the result is a single article, for example, or a list of articles.

With a click of the mouse, you can access a comprehensive knowledge base that you collected. Instructors can use InfoTrac InfoMarks to generate reading lists, study guides, bibliographies, electronic journal directories, and more. Students can, too, to share their research with fellow students, study groups, instructors, and others.

For more information and access to the InfoMark Online Learning Center, click the InfoMark button 🛈 on a BCRC search results page—or visit the InfoMarks Web site at **www.gale.com/infomarks**.

Business & Company
RESOURCE CENTER

PL: 91 1/8 DIS: 27 7/8 K

GALE CENGAGE LEARNING

Using Your Research . . .

The Business & Company Resource Center is a powerful research tool that has an important purpose: ensuring your academic and career success. Your instructor will use the BCRC as a major component of the syllabus and assign BCRC-facilitated reading and research projects for your analysis, either individually or in groups. These assignments will typically be in a supportive role to a case study analysis, for background research into class topics—even for writing your own case studies, the goal of various new learning techniques designed to engage students fully in their educational experience and ease their transition to the workplace.

In the following sections, the general guidelines are given for case study analysis and using the BCRC. Guidelines are also supplied for properly citing your BCRC sources using APA style.

CASE ANALYSIS

Students of biology, chemistry, and the physical sciences learn their fields through practicing and experimenting with theories and materials in the laboratory. As a student of management, organizational behavior, human resource management, and other business-related disciplines, your laboratory exists in the issues presented by your instructor, your course materials (e.g., Harvard Business School cases), and by your own research endeavors. Cases provide the opportunity to experiment with real organizations in the classroom setting. The Business & Company Resource Center enhances this process both at an analytical level and in the authoring of case studies (see the guidelines in "Writing a Case Study"). Below are a set of standard steps for an individual or class group to perform a case analysis; the BCRC resources that typically apply are indicated with their tab names in bold.

1. History, development, and growth of the organization—**Histories**.

2. Identification of the internal strengths and weaknesses of the organization—**News/Magazines; Investment Reports; Financials; Suits and Claims**

3. Nature of the external environment surrounding the organization—**News/Magazines; Investment Reports; Financials; Rankings; Suits and Claims; Industry Overview**

4. SWOT (Strengths, Weaknesses, Opportunities, and Threats) analysis—**News/Magazines; Investment Reports; Financials; Suits and Claims; Industry Overview.**

5. The type of corporate-level strategy pursued by the organization—**News/Magazines**.

6. The nature of the organization's business-level strategy—**News/Magazines**.

7. The organization's structure and control systems and how they match its strategy—**Company Profile; News/Magazines**.

8. Recommendations for the organization—**All tabs**.

Management, business, and organizational behavior studies like any field, can be learned at three different levels: memorization, understanding, and application. Memorization is the lowest level of learning and involves the simple recitation of facts and simple concepts. Understanding involves deeper learning. It includes the ability to deal with relationships among concepts and to deal with concepts in different contexts. Application is the highest level of learning. Concepts have to be very well understood to apply

Harvard Business School

9-800-305
Rev. December 19, 2000

Staples.com

As she walked up to the main entrance of Staples Inc.'s headquarters in Framingham, MA, Kelly Mahoney thought that the building — where, to her surprise, Staples' dotcom division was located — looked even more imposing than she had imagined. As the chief marketing officer at Arnold Direct, Mahoney was a skilled direct marketing strategist, and was looking to parlay her experience into a new opportunity on the Internet (See Exhibit 1 for Kelly Mahoney's resume). She was weighing several opportunities, including an offer from Staples.com, the online division of the office products giant.

From her due diligence and from past project work with Staples Inc., Kelly was familiar with Staples' reputation for excellent customer service, an innovative and entrepreneurial culture, and a commitment to serving the needs of small business owners. However, Kelly wanted to learn more about the online division's strategy. Did Staples.com have a plan to claim the number one industry position? Would this job offer her the best personal and financial rewards?

Introduction to a Harvard case study about Staples.com

them to the real world. Mastery of concepts sufficient to solve problems or to diagnose real organizational situations is a significant accomplishment. Learning to understand and apply concepts can be effectively and rewardingly accomplished through case study.

Cases—and the complementary readings and research that the BCRC makes possible—do not replace your textbook and lectures. These provide a theoretical background. The material in a casebook and the data and articles in the BCRC database are supplements; they extend the learning process to the real world. The goal of studying management, organizational behavior, human resource management, and the like with cases is to enable you to apply what is taught from a textbook to a real situation—a reconciliation of theory with life. Managers use theories and models in their day-to-day management of organizations. Often these models are intuitive and implicit. Sometimes they are explicit, just as in textbooks. Whatever the nature of the theory or model they use, managers must react to situations relying on past experience and acquired skills to analyze and assess the issues and arrive at a solution. Case study (using such resources as the BCRC) develops your skill in analyzing problems and generating solutions based on your understanding of the theories and models of organization processes and behavior.

Your course may involve reading, commenting, and even writing a wide variety of cases. The cases can be categorized by the educational objective of the instructor and the role of you, the student. The first type of case learning is theory application/illustration. In this type of case, the problem or issue outlined in the situation has usually been solved, and it is your responsibility to analyze the outcome and its consequences. Cases selected for this type of analysis may not emphasize any problem, but present real-life situations that can be used to explain and illustrate theories and models of management, organizational behavior, or human resource management. The facts in the case may be focused toward specific theories, but seemingly irrelevant material will also be included. Sometimes you will be asked to evaluate the solution in the case and to propose an alternative solution if necessary. The second type of case educational objective is problem analysis. Cases used for this objective may be relatively complex. Your role will be to analyze and interpret the situation. You will have to sort out the facts of the case, determine the cause-and-effect relationships, and design a solution and plan for implementation. The primary goal is to solve the problem. The illustration of theories and models is not the primary goal of the case, but theories and models will be used to help identify alternatives and justify your solution.

As you develop your analytical and conceptual skills through the case method, you will be able to master the understanding and use of theories of management, organizational behavior, and human resource management. Many of the cases combine more than one objective. A specific case might be used to practice the application of theory or to engage you in the identification and solution of the problem. For any of these materials to enrich your learning experience requires your involvement. An integral part of the learning process is your commitment to preparing the analysis or application and becoming involved in class discussion. Remember, the cases serve a dual purpose: to develop your skills in problem solution and to increase your ability to apply theory to real situations.

WRITING A CASE STUDY ANALYSIS—GUIDELINES

1. The Introduction includes what products or services the organization produces; its history; its successes and problems; the focus of your analysis, that is, what you will discuss and in what order.

2. The Strategic Analysis section typically utilizes some analytical model (e.g., SWOT analysis) to develop your narrative about the problems the organization faces.

3. In the third part, your Solutions and Recommendations are presented in a way that follows from the presentation of the problems you analyzed in the Strategic Analysis section.

CITING SOURCES IN THE BCRC*

College instructors typically require that students follow a specific method of presenting and listing outside sources. Your instructor may have a particular style of citation that he or she prefers, such as CMS recommended by the Chicago Manual of Style, MLA developed by the Modern Language Association, and the APA style by the American Psychological Association. Each style is suitable for citing the sources you find in the BCRC database.

Many students find citing sources the most challenging aspect of writing a case study or research paper. The purpose of documenting your sources, however, serves several important purposes:

- *Citations prevent allegations of plagiarism.* Plagiarism is a form of theft when a person presents someone else's facts, words, or ideas as his or her own. Copying and pasting materials found on the Web may not seem like a crime, but the typical punishment for submitting a paper with plagiarized material is automatically failing the course. In some academic settings, it can also mean expulsion.

- *Citations support the thesis.* A citation in a research paper is not unlike expert testimony introduced into a courtroom.

- *Citations refer readers to other sources.* Citations alert readers where they can find more information about the information conveyed in the research paper or case study.

Certain kinds of quotations that have entered the language as common sense phrases, such as quotes from Shakespeare plays and the Bible, as well as generally accessible information such as the birth and death years of a public figure, do not need to be cited. However, in most instances, you have to acknowledge the use of outside material for the following examples:

- *Direct quotations.* Whenever you quote a source word for word, you must place it in quotation marks and cite its source.

- *Indirect quotations or paraphrases.* Even if you do not copy a source but state the author's ideas in your own words, you must cite the source. Changing a few words or summarizing a page of text into a few sentences does not alter the fact that you are using someone else's ideas.

- *Specific facts, statistics, and numbers.* Data will only be credible and acceptable if you present the source. Statistics only make credible evidence if readers trust their source.

---

* Adapted from Connelly, M. (2003). *The Sundance Reader*, 3rd ed. Boston: Thomson Heinle.

- *Graphs, charts, and other visual aids.* Indicate the source of any graphic you reproduce. You must also cite the source for information you use to create a visual display.

APA Style for BCRC Sources

For citing the sources you find using the BCRC, a standard or modified APA style is recommended. APA style is used in social sciences such as psychology, sociology, and economics. Increasing, it is now also being applied to related disciplines, including strategic management, organizational design, and so on. The following guidelines apply:

- The sources cited in your case study should be listed in a separate section titled "References" or "Bibliography" (to list works used but not cited).

- Sources alphabetized by last name or title.

An example of a book listed in APA style in a case study reference list:

> Carroll, A., & Buchholtz, A. (2003). *Business & Society: Ethics and Stakeholder Management*, 5th ed. Mason, OH: Thomson South-Western.

If it were cited in text:

> The tobacco industry is an example of an industry that is experience allegations of power abuse (Carroll & Buchholtz, 2003).

When the source is named in text:

> Carroll and Buchholtz see the tobacco industry as an industry that is experiencing allegations of power abuse (2003).

Finding the information you need to cite is easy in a BCRC article webpage:

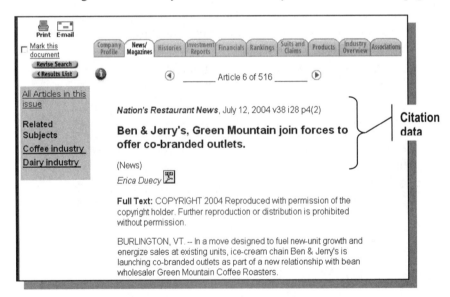

You would cite this article about Ben & Jerry's Homemade Ice Cream in an APA-style bibliography as shown:

> Duecy, E. (2004, July 12). Ben & Jerry's, Green Mountain join forces to offer co-branded outlets. *Nation's Restaurant News*, 38, 4.

In text:

> Ben & Jerry's Homemade Ice Cream has a strategy that does not rule out cooperative ventures, for example, with the coffee roaster Green Mountain (Duecy, 2004).

Source named in text:

> Duecy (2004) noted Ben & Jerry's strategy of cooperative ventures with the coffee roaster Green Mountain.

For articles without an author, such as this brief article in *Dairy Foods* about Ben & Jerry's Rock the Vote initiative shown below, you would use the title.

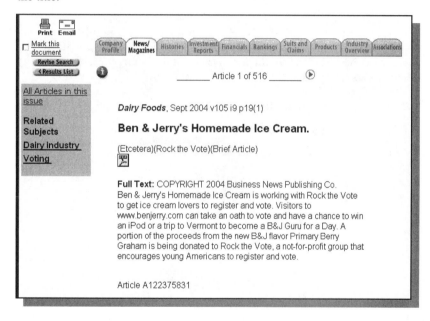

Bibliography entry:

> Ben & Jerry's Homemade Ice Cream. (2004). *Dairy Foods,* 105 (9), 19.

In text:

> Ben & Jerry's Homemade Ice Cream is participating in the Rock the Vote movement ("Ben & Jerry's," 2004).

If source is named in text:

> *Dairy Foods* (2004) noted that Ben & Jerry's participated in Rock the Vote during election year 2004.

Citing BCRC in an APA-style Citation

When you cite a BCRC source, you should not only include the bibliographical information about the original source, you should also indicate that you are citing a source that is reproduced in the BCRC database as shown:

> Duecy, E. (2004, July 12). Ben & Jerry's, Green Mountain join forces to offer co-branded outlets. *Nation's Restaurant News*, 38, 4. Reproduced in Business and Company Resource Center. Farmington Hills, MI: Gale Group. 2004. http://galenet.galegroup.com/servlet/BCRC.

If your instructor requires that you add the BCRC article number to your APA-style citation, you may add it in brackets as shown:

> *Dairy Foods.* (2004). Ben & Jerry's Homemade Ice Cream. *Dairy Foods,* 105 (9), 19. Reproduced in Business and Company Resource Center. Farmington Hills, MI: Gale Group. 2004. http://galenet.galegroup.com/servlet/BCRC [Article A122375831].

For more about the APA style guidelines, refer to the official manual, *Publication Manual of the American Psychological Association*, 5th edition and visit the APA website at **http://www.apastyle.org/**. Many university libraries also have APA style guide webpages.

Sources Available in the BCRC

To find out more about the databases that are available in the Business and Company Resource Center, click link at the top of any BCRC webpage, which includes *American Wholesalers and Distributors Directory, International Directory of Company Histories, Ward's Business Directory of U.S. Private and Public Companies*, and so on.